FEASTS OF
JEHOVAH

FEASTS OF JEHOVAH

by
John Ritchie

KREGEL PUBLICATIONS
Grand Rapids, Michigan 49501

Feasts of Jehovah by John Ritchie, Copyright
© 1982 by Kregel Publications, a division of
Kregel, Inc., under special arrangements with John
Ritchie, Ltd., Kilmarnock, Scotland. All rights
reserved.

First Kregel Publications edition 1982
Reprinted 1986

Library of Congress Cataloging in Publication Data

Ritchie, John.
  Feasts of Jehovah.

  Reprint. Originally published: Kilmarnock,
Scotland : J. Ritchie.
  1. Fasts and feasts in the Bible—Typology.
2. Typology (Theology) I. Title.
BM690.R48   1982   221.6'4   82-182
ISBN 0-8254-3613-3 (pbk.)   AACR2

Printed in the United States of America

CONTENTS

Foreword .... *vii*

Introduction *9*

The Redeemed of the Lord 11

The Seven Feasts 18

The Sabbath 24

The Passover 28

Feast of Unleavened Bread 33

Feast of Firstfruits 39

Pentecost, the Feast of Weeks 45

The Present Interval 53

Feast of Trumpets 56

Day of Atonement 60

Feast of Tabernacles 67

Appendices *72*

Diagram of the Feasts *78*

FOREWORD

These feasts of Jehovah mirror the Truth and reflect our blessed Lord, like the waves of a beautiful, blue lake mirror and reflect the shimmering light of the sun and the glories of the sky. In this classic, concise treatment of the feasts, John Ritchie brings the reader to the central meaning of each observance. These chapters blend together with accurate preparation and acute presentation.

The busy pastor, missionary and evangelist, the pressured college teacher, the searching student and the earnest seeker for Truth will all find this little volume refreshing and stimulating.

Feast of Jehovah is actually part of an excellent brief but beautiful trilogy. The reader will want to certainly complete his journey from Egypt to Canaan by reading *Feasts of Jehovah, The Tabernacle* and *From Egypt to Canaan*. All three volumes would make a very interesting study series for a Bible study class, mid-week services or a series of Sunday School lessons. In whatever way you use this little book, you will find it to be a spiritual feast.

Arnold J. Fair

INTRODUCTION

(LEVITICUS 23)

THIS chapter gives an account of the seven great feasts, which Jehovah commanded His people Israel to annually observe in the land of Canaan.

It contains in typical language, a record of God's dealings with man in grace, from the death of Christ to His millennial kingdom, and to the eternal glory and rest, which lie beyond it.

It is also a prophecy, and a foreshadowing of some great events of the future, part of which have since been fulfilled, and part of which are yet to be.

The " Feasts of Jehovah " all pointed onward to subjects of eternal interest ; subjects on which the mind and heart of God—Father, Son, and Holy Spirit—had been engaged before the world was, and which in due time and order, were to take their places in that marvellous chain of events, which when completed, will shew the infinite wisdom and love of God, in all His purposes of grace toward the sons of men.

They are each a " shadow of things to come," of which Christ is the " body " (Col. 2:17) or substance ; foreshadowings of His peerless Person, and infinitely precious work, over which all true believers delight to meditate, on which by faith they feed, and which they find to be the strength and joy of their spiritual life.

May our souls be fed, our spiritual strength and vigour increased, and our hearts drawn God-ward, Christ-ward and heaven-ward, as we meditate for a little together on this great chapter.

There are many of the subjects that will pass before us, which will be familiar to those who have known the Lord, and found their delight in His Word for many years. For the truths of this typical chapter are all cardinal truths of our most holy faith, the very foundations of Christianity, the solid rocks on which the faith and hope of saints all through the ages has rested ; which, though old are never new, and their re-stating always welcome to those who have known them longest and best. And it may be there are little ones of the flock of Christ, and young ones of the family of God, to whom these great and precious themes will be a means of establishing, and strengthening, in a day of perplexity and conflicting sounds, a day in which the enemy, no longer content with attacking the outposts, is seeking to carry the battle to the very center of the camp. His great business now is to assail if he can, the foundations of the faith.

The Redeemed of the Lord

" Happy art thou, O Israel ; who is like unto thee,
O people saved by the Lord ", (Deut. 33:29).

" The Children of Israel, a people near unto Him "
(Ps. 148:14).

" No longer far from Him, but now
By ' precious blood ' made nigh ;
' Accepted ' in the Well-Beloved,
Near to God's heart we lie."

BEFORE looking at the feasts in the order in which they are here recorded, it may be well to pause for a moment, and reflect upon the history of the people to whom these instructions were given, and to consider where, and at what period of their history, these commandments from Jehovah reached them.

The preceding book—the Book of Exodus—opens with a picture of this people in Egyptian bondage, serving Pharaoh and his gods. No " Feasts of Jehovah," no holy convocations, or times of rejoicing were known by them there. They were slaves and idolaters. This shews man in his natural state: unregenerate, unconverted man, away from God, in, and of the world, serving Satan, its " god " and " prince ". But to this down-trodden people, redemption and deliverance came. They were brought out from Egypt, separated from its people and its idolatries, to become the

chosen people of Jehovah. " Ye have seen what I did unto
the Egyptians, and how I bare you on eagle's wings, and
brought you unto MYSELF: " (Exodus 19:4). They were
delivered from the rule and authority of Pharaoh, to be
Jehovah's " peculiar treasure," a people " near unto Him "
(Psa. 148:14)   a people " not reckoned among the
nations," but dwelling alone (Num. 23:9). with Jehovah
in their midst, shielding, protecting, and ruling over them.
No wonder that Moses, the man of God, in taking his
farewell of them, as they encamped on the last stage of
their wilderness journey, uttered the ever-memorable
words—" Happy art thou, O Israel : who is like unto
thee, O people saved by the Lord "   (Deut. 33:29).
And the position, and the blessings of Israel as the redeemed
of Jehovah, are but shadows of the still higher and wealthier
place into which all believers of this age are brought
" in Christ," as described in the glowing words of the
apostle—" Blessed be the God and Father of our Lord
Jesus Christ, who hath blessed us with *all spiritual blessings*
in *heavenly places* in Christ " (Eph. 1:3).

Less than this would have satisfied us—to be delivered
from hell and judgment, was all that *we* desired in our
unconverted days-but less than this could not satisfy our
God, or fulfil the desires of His heart. His purpose was
to have a people near unto Him, a family around Himself,
all comely in His eyes, all " holy and without blame
before Him in love " (Eph. 1:4).

It was after Israel had been brought completely out
from Egypt, and gathered around Jehovah in the wilderness, with His presence in their midst, His cloud hovering
over them, that He gave them these commandments concerning His feasts. He was able then to reveal to them
what was in His heart, and to invite them to share with

Him, the great things which had been the subjects of His
thoughts from eternal ages. This chapter would have
been of no use to them in Egypt ; other interests occupied
them while there ; but now, alone in the desert, separated
unto God the subjects of His redeeming grace and power,
He was able to tell out His heart's desire. And they, no
longer occupied with Egypt's sins and follies, no longer
groaning for deliverance, but now standing in the full
enjoyment of Jehovah's salvation, were able to hear and
respond to these desires of His heart.

Notice, too, they are " Feasts (or " set feasts," see R.V.,
the word used signifying " to meet by appointment ") of
Jehovah." or " Jehovah's Feasts." Jehovah was the Host,
His people were the guests. He ordained these feasts as
celebrations of His own joy, His own delight, in the great
events to which they pointed, and of which they were the
foreshadowing types. Yes, they were *His* feasts, and they
let us understand in what *His* delights and enjoyments are
found. The various feasts, as they pass before us, now
read and understood in the light of their antitypes, tell out
what has afforded the God of heaven, the blessed Trinity—
Father, Son, and Spirit,—joy and delight for ages past, and
what will still supply the joy of heaven in ages yet to come.
How poor and miserable are the subjects that occasion
mirth and gladness among the sons of men compared with
these ! And how soon they fade away, and are forgotten !
But heaven's enjoyments last ; they do not lose their
charm. The Person and the work of Christ retain their
fragrance, and continue to yield to all heaven an Object to
gaze upon, and a theme to sing of. After earth's songs
have all been sung : its joys all ended : its mirth passed
away : heaven's " Hallelujah Psalm " will continue to be
sung by radiant hosts, in immortal youth around the throne.

And " Jehovah's set Feasts " were " holy convocations,"
that is " calling together " of His people. He did not keep
all His joys to Himself : He shared them with His redeemed
people.   He called them together around Himself to be
joint-partakers with Him of His joy.   How wonderful is
this ! But how much more so, is God's present grace to
His heavenly people.   Our God is not a lonely Being—like
the God of the Unitarian and of the Mohammedan—He
is a God of fellowship.   He delights to have His people
sharing His joys, and finding their delights in Christ, in
Whom His own are all found.   This is fellowship.   This
is that to which the saints have been called : to share God's
thoughts of Christ : to find their rest with Him in Christ.
This is our calling : it ought to be our experience and
enjoyment.   Does the world deprive us of it ? Do earthly
things so occupy and engross our thoughts and affections,
that the things of God and of Christ get little attention ?
Does business and worldly cares so monopolize our days
and hours, that there is no energy, no time left, and, alas
but little *heart* to think of, and delight in God, and His
Christ ?

Individually, the saints are called to have fellowship
with the Father and the Son (1 John 1:3), and collectively,
the Church—the " called out " and " called together "
company of God's saints, is called unto *the* fellowship of
God's Son—" Jesus Christ our Lord " (1 Cor. 1:9), all of
which most clearly show, how delightful it is to God, to
jointly-share with His people, all that gives joy and gladness
to His own heart.

Now just in passing, and in contrast to all this, let us
look at what we find in John 2:13; 5:1; 7:2. In the days
of the Lord on earth, these feasts were still being observed
by the Jewish people in the city of Jerusalem, the

place where God's temple stood. Crowds from all parts
of the country came up to Jerusalem to keep the Passover,
the feast of Pentecost, and the feast of Tabernacles. But
what does the Lord call them ? No longer His feasts, but
" feasts of the Jews." The outward form was there, but
Jehovah's joy in them had ceased. Speaking of them in
an earlier day, He said—" *Your* new moons and *your*
appointed feasts My soul hateth, they are a trouble to Me.
I am weary to bear them " (Isa. 1:14). And this because
of the formal manner in which a defiled and corrupted
people observed them. And surely, beloved children of
God, we may learn from this, the searching and solemn
lesson, that when the heart is away from God, the hands
defiled by sin, the feet ceasing to walk in the truth, an
empty form of worship is only a farce and a sham. How
much there is in our day, of great account in the eyes of
men, highly esteemed and loudly praised, which a holy
God finds a weariness, which His soul hates, and with
which He will not connect His Name. Let us keep a
jealous watch on our hearts—the source of all departure
from God is there—lest of us He may have to say, " My
soul shall have no pleasure in him " (Heb. 10:38).

And so desirous was Jehovah that His people should
approach Him three times each year at these "set feasts,"
happy and without care, that He pledged His word to look
well to their earthly interests, to care for their wives, their
children, and their land, all the time they were at Jerusalem
keeping His feasts. We all know how impossible it is to
rejoice before the Lord, and to worship Him joyfully, when
household cares and business worries, are pressing like a
burden on the mind. No doubt Jehovah knew, that when
the " males " of Israel went up to keep the feasts, leaving
all behind them, the thought might often rise to disturb

them—" What if the Philistines invade the country while we are away, and take possession of our fields " ? And so He gave them a special promise that during their absence no one should be allowed to take away or even desire their possessions. " Neither shall any man desire thy land when thou shalt go to appear before the Lord thy God thrice in the year" (Exod. 34:24). Blessed be his Name! And the the same God who says, " Gather my saints together unto Me," and forbids His people to forsake " the assembling of themselves together " (Heb. 10:25) now, will surely make it His care to see that those who render hearty obedience to His command, shall not be losers for time or eternity by so doing. Yet, alas ! how often a passing shower, a slight ailment, a domestic duty, is sufficient excuse for absence at the Lord's Supper, and for neglect of the worship of God. But the promise of God abides the same, and all who give the Lord His due, will find it fulfilled. "Them that honour Me, I will honour." "Seek ye *first* the kingdom of God, and His righteousness"—that is, give God His due, make His demands your first concern —" and all these things shall be added unto you".

And as Jehovah was the host, and His people only the guests, the whole arrangements, the time, the place, the ordering of the feasts, were all undertaken by Himself alone. Nothing was left to the people's vote. Divine legislation provided for the whole. Happy had it been for the people of God then had they been content with the Divine commandments concerning their assemblings, and added nothing to them. And happy surely will it be with Christians now, if in their church order, and their worship, they cleave to, and follow the Word of God. Had this been done, creeds and confessions, with their resulting divisions and barriers, had been unknown. And all God's saints, as in days of old, would be found of one heart and soul, guided by one Book, governed by one Head, themselves happy and peaceful, a power and a testimony for God in the midst of an evil world.

The Seven Feasts

*" **These are the set feasts of Jehovah** " (Lev. 23:4,* R.V.*).*
" A shadow of the things to come " (Col. 2:17).

> *" Blessed table, where the Lord*
> *Sets for us His choicest cheer :*
> *Angels hath no feast like this,*
> *Angels serve, but cannot share."*

BEFORE proceeding to consider the various feasts, and to gather the great doctrinal and practical lessons God has designed them to teach us, I would ask you to look at this diagram (see beginning of book), on which these feasts appear tabulated in their order.

They are seven in number, or, if we include the Sabbath, eight. The Sabbath must be considered separately from the rest. It stands by itself, alike in its character and in the frequency of its observance. It was observed weekly : the rest of the feasts annually. It could be kept at home, while all the others must be observed at " the place " which Jehovah had chosen in which to place His Name (Deut. 12:14; 16:6). And you will notice, that the chapter opens with the words—" These are the feasts (or "set feasts") of Jehovah," Deut. 12:2. Then after giving commandment about the Sabbath, in verse 3 the statement —"These are the set feasts of Jehovah"—occurs again, making as it were, a fresh beginning. And then the seven feasts are described without a fresh repetition of

these words. Thus, while the Sabbath stands alone, the
other seven follow in sequence, and have a certain relation
to each other. Although the Sabbath is first mentioned, it
is last in being fulfilled. The rest of the feasts have their
fulfilment, in time, while all that the Sabbath bespeaks,
can only be known in its fulness in Eternity.

The Seven Feasts may be divided into two sections of
four and three.

The Passover, the Feast of Unleavened Bread, the
Feast of First-fruits, and Pentecost, followed each other
closely. Then there was an interval of four months, during
which there was no " feast of Jehovah " and no " holy
convocation " of the people at Jerusalem—a long pause,
as it were, between the feast of Pentecost and the blowing
of Trumpets, during which no fresh call from Jehovah to
His people was heard. This is significant and instructive.
The meaning of it seems to be, that the truths foreshadowed
in the first four feasts are all connected with the *present*
age, and the out-calling and place of those who form the
heavenly people of the Lord, the body of Christ, while
the last three feasts foreshadow future mercies and times
of blessing which are in store for Jehovah's *earthly* people,
as well as his heavenly people of this present time. In
other words, the first four speak *of* and *to* the Church, the
body of Christ, while the latter three speak also of Jehovah's
future dealings with His earthly people, Israel, the seed of
Abraham, the nation of His choice, who will then be again
gathered to their own land, in covenant relation with God
in the latter days for earthly blessing, under Messiah their
king. It will be seen that He who ordained these feasts as
celebrations of His own joy in the great events to which
they pointed, and invited His redeemed and chosen people
to gather together and share His joys with Him, has fulfilled

to the letter what has already come to pass. And this surely warrants the expectation that He will as surely in His own due time fulfil what yet remains. For the purposes of God stand fast, and can never be disannulled by the perversities and failures of men.. How a chapter like this, so full of the glorious Gospel of God, so replete with types and teachings on the foundations of the faith, all so clearly the inspiration of the eternal God, speaking of things beforehand which He has purposed should come to pass, should confirm and strengthen our faith in the sacred and infallible Word of God—the Book around, and against which, the great battle waged by infidelity and so-called " Science " rages, seeking to undo faith's hold, and raise doubts and question as to its credibility. But the words of the Lord are pure words. They will stand to be examined with miscroscopic care. And the more they are thus examined in the fear of God, the stronger will the evidences appear on every page that they are what they claim to be, the *Theopneusta* (2 Tim. 3:16), the God-breathed words of Him who cannot lie.

Three times in the year all the males of Israel were commanded to appear before the Lord their God ; at the Passover, the Feast of Weeks or Pentecost, and the Feast of Tabernacles (see Exodus 23:14-17) in the place where the Lord had placed His Name (Deut, 16:16). With what joy and gladness the thousands of Israel, of all the tribes, gathered from all parts of the goodly land, assembled there to rejoice before Jehovah, and to give Him back His portion, out of the fulness of blessing He had given them (Deut. 16:17). The little cluster of Psalms 122-134, called " Songs of Degress," are believed to have been chanted by the crowds of joyful pilgrims, as they journeyed toward the city of the Great King—that Jerusalem, which

was " beautiful for situation, the joy of the whole earth,"
in the palaces of which God was known " for a refuge "
(Psa. 48:2-3). While the people of the Lord were
right in heart, they rejoiced in these assemblings to the
full, and were glad as they said one to another, " Let us go
into the house of the Lord " (Psa. 122:1).   But when they
got away in heart from their God, they found His commandments grievous, and soon neglected them. How dim
the fine gold had become, in the days of Malachi when
none would open a door or kindle a fire in God's house for
nought, when the blind and the lame were offered in
sacrifice, and when Jehovah's worship and service had
become " a weariness". The answer to this in our day
is easily found. When saints are right in heart with their
God, in the dew of spiritual youth, nothing is deemed too
costly or too great for Him. The heart's song then is—

> " Nought that I have mine own I call,
>   I hold it for the Giver ;
> My heart, my strength, my life, my all,
>   Are His, and His for ever."

The feet are swift in running His errands, the hands are
diligent doing His work ; joy and gladness shine in the
very countenance. And blessed it is to know that this
condition may be carried with us to the journey's end.
There is no necessity and no provisions made for decline.
The saint may be fresh and green even in old age, like the
palm-tree, ever yielding fruit.

When we come to the New Testament times, we do
not find the many feasts of former times continued. There
is only one feast given to the church, one holy convocation
of saints of the present age. That feast is the Lord's
Supper. That gathering is the " ecclesia," the assembled
church. Just as the seven feasts of Jehovah pointed

onward to Christ, and were foreshadowings of redemption and glory, so the Lord's Supper looks backward to the Cross, and onward to the glory. It is the memorial of Christ's death, and the pledge of His coming again. It embraces within itself all that was typified in these seven feasts of Jehovah.

The bread and wine are the memorials of Christ's death. This is the answer to *The Passover*.

The Communion of Saints in holiness and love, gathered around that table feeding together on Christ, is the answer to the *The Feast of Unleavened* Bread.

The One Body of Christ formed and in-dwelt by the Spirit of God ; the gathered saints " builded together for an habitation of God in the Spirit " (Eph. 2:22) ; the Spirit present to guide in worship and ministry, to take of the things of Christ and present them to the gathered worshippers, answers to *Pentecost*.

The feast continued " till He come " directs the eye of hope to the great and glorious future, viz., the Coming of the Lord to awaken the sleeping saints, to change the living, and to gather all together around Himself. The Judgment Seat to review and reward all faithful service for the Lord : the bright beams of Millennial glory : the glorious reign of Christ and His people over a peaceful world, anticipate the fulfilment of the *Feast of Trumpets*, the *Atonement* and the joyful *Feast of Tabernacles* for the heavenly people, while their meaning and their message to the " blinded " earthly people are unheard and unheeded.

And thus on the first day of the week, the saints assembled around their Lord, gathered in His peerless Name to break the bread and drink the wine for a remembrance of Him, meditate upon, and pass in spirit through all these wondrous scenes which are the strength and joy of the new man. May we ever have hearts to enjoy these privileges worthily. And as one who knew them well, sang long ago, and has left for other hearts and lips, may we truly sing—

> " To Calvary, Lord, in spirit now
>   Our joyful souls repair,
> To dwell upon Thy dying love,
>   And taste its sweetness there.
>
> Thy sympathies and hopes are ours,
>   We long, O Lord to see
> Creation all below, above,
>   Redeemed and blessed by Thee."

The Sabbath

" The seventh day is the Sabbath of rest " (Lev. 23:3).

" There remaineth therefore a Sabbath-rest for the people of God "
(Heb. 4:9 R.V.).

" That rest secure from ill,
No cloud of grief ere stains,
Unfailing praise each heart doth fill,
And love eternal reigns."

THE Sabbath, standing as it does in the forefront of
this great typical chapter, has a place and a character
of its own.   It was observed weekly all through the
year, while the other feasts were in progress and other-
wise. It had an existence long before any of them, even as
far back as Gen. chap. ii., and all along it had been bringing
its weekly day of rest to the weary sons of toil.   The
Sabbath was " a shadow of things to come " (Col. 2:17),
a sign and pledge of that Sabbath-keeping which remains,
the eternal rest of God and of His people, when time shall
be no more, and when the redeemed of all ages and dis-
pensations shall enter into full and perfect rest as promised
in the word—" There remaineth therefore a Sabbath-rest
for the people of God " (Heb. 4:9, R.V.).

In an eternity past, before the earth was formed, or
the mountains brought forth (Psa. 90:2), God—Father,
Son, and Spirit—kept Sabbath.   After the six days work
as recorded in Gen. 1, again God—Father, Son, and

Spirit rested. The first paradisical Sabbath was the rest of God—" He rested from all His work " which He had " created and made " (Gen. 2:3). His creative work was perfect, therefore the operation of His hand ceased, and He rested. And as a memorial of His creative power, the seventh day was set apart from the other days of the week. In what manner it was distinguished and observed before the fall, we have no account. But the Creator's rest was bound up with the work of which it was the memorial. That work was marred by the entrance of sin and the fall of man, from his primal state. And when Adam fell, his kingdom lost its original perfectness. The work of creation being thus marred, the rest connected with it was broken. The Sabbath could no longer be the memorial of a *present* rest of the Creator in His work. It was continued as the foreshadowing of another rest, based upon *redemption* which in mercy God would introduce, a rest not dependent upon the goodness of the creature, but upon the infinite worth and perfect work of a Redeemer. Thus it was that the Sabbath became a " shadow of Christ," pointing forward to Him who was to come, on whose Person and Work a new creation was to be framed, and a new rest found, which Satan would be unable to overthrow, or sin to mar. This was the work spoken of by the Lord Jesus, when He was accused of breaking the Sabbath. " My Father worketh hitherto, and I work " (John 5:17), said the living Lord. And ere He yielded up His spirit on Calvary, He was able to say triumphantly, " It is finished " (John 19:30). It was to this, that Israel's Sabbaths and days of rest pointed : they were the shadows of the rest which was to be found by God and His people in redemption. The final and complete fulfilment of this Sabbath will be in the Eternal Rest, when in resurrection bodies, in new heavens and a new earth wherein dwelleth righteousness, God's will shall be perfectly done, and God Himself will be all in all. Even now, flowing from the death of Christ, there are, and will be, pledges and foretastes of that rest. To the burdened *sinner*, the Lord Jesus says, " Come unto Me, all ye that labour and are heavy laden, and I will give you rest " (Matt. 11:28). And all who hear and obey that call, are even now able to sing—

> " I came to Jesus as I was,
>   Weary and worn and sad ;
> I found in Him a resting-place,
>   And He has made me glad."

To the saint, there is a further and deeper rest, as expressed in the words that follow :—" Take My yoke upon you and learn of Me ; for I am meek and lowly in heart : and ye shall find rest to your souls" (Matt. 11:29). This is found in obedience to Christ as Lord, in submission to His will, in bowing under His yoke. This also is a present blessing.

To the servant wearied *in*, but not *of* His Master's work, how sweetly come the words—" Come ye yourselves apart, and *rest* a while " : and there, alone in the presence of His Master and Lord, far from the bustle and the toil, he finds rest and refreshing, and comes forth freshly-girded for his toil.

And to those who have left us and are " with Christ " (Phil 1:23),   there has come a further instalment of the promised rest. Their conflicts are over, their days of toil are ended, and they rest " at home with their Lord " in paradise (see 2 Cor. 5:8 ; Luke 23:43).

The millennium will be a further stage of this God-given rest. During the thousand years of Messiah's reign, Satan will be bound, and the groan of creation will cease.

The prophetic word will then be fulfilled—" The whole earth is at rest, and is quiet: they break forth into singing" (Isa. 14:7). The noise of war, the clash of arms, the cry of the oppressed, the wail of sorrow will cease, and under the peaceful beams of the Sun of Righteousness, the benign rule of the Prince of Peace, the wearied earth will keep its Sabbath. But this, blessed as it is, is not the *final* rest. Sin will lurk beneath. Satan although bound, will not be destroyed. There will be a last great outburst of man's sin and Satan's rage (Rev. 20:7), which judgment from heaven will quell and end. Then will come the eternal rest, that unending Sabbath-keeping of God and His people, the Rest of Eternity.

The Passover

" Thou shalt sacrifice the passover at even, at the going down of the sun, at the season that thou camest forth out of Egypt " (Deut. 16:6).

" Christ our Passover is sacrificed for us. Therefore let us keep the feast " (1 Cor. 5:7-8).

> *" No bone of Thee was broken*
> *Thou spotless Paschal Lamb !*
> *Of life and peace a token,*
> *To us who know Thy Name :*
> *The Head for all the members,*
> *The curse, the vengeance bore,*
> *And God, our God, remembers*
> *His people's sins no more."*

THE Passover was the first of Jehovah's set feasts. It was observed on the fourteenth day of the first month—the month of Abib (Deut. 16:1). It was the great memorial of redemption and deliverance from Egypt, observed from year to year. Of its typical meaning we are left in no doubt, for the Spirit's inspired commentary is—" Christ our Passover is sacrificed for us " (1 Cor. 5:7). The paschal Lamb was a type of Christ. Each time it was sacrificed, it pointed onward to Him who was to come, the Lamb of God, through whose atoning death, sin was to be put away, and believing sinners brought nigh to God.

When the Passover was first given to Israel, the Israelites were slaves to Pharaoh the Egyptian king, and idolators

serving Egypt's gods.   They were thus amenable to the
righteous judgment of God.   But in mercy that stroke was
averted, and they were " passed over".   The Divine
assurance was given. "When I see the *blood* I will pass over
you " (Exod. 12:13).   That blood, was the blood of the
slain lamb.   The stroke had fallen on a spotless victim.
The lamb died that they might live.   The blood appropriated : sprinkled with hyssop on the lintel and side-posts
of the door, secured immunity from death.   The word of
Jehovah gave them assurance of safety.*   The blood of the
lamb was thus the foundation of their new relation to
Jehovah, as His people.   Redemption by the blood of the
lamb was their meritorious title to all the privileges and
blessings which they afterwards received and enjoyed as
the people of God.   The blood was the foundation of
everything.   The day on which it was shed and sprinkled
marked the beginning of their history as Jehovah's
redeemed people.   It was their birthday as a new and
separate nation ; their days and months were counted, the
entire calendar of their sacred year was made up anew,
from that day (Exod. 12:2).   This shows how Redemption
and Regeneration are linked together in the thoughts of
God.   To trust Christ's blood is to be " born again."   The
six months of the year which had already run their course,
were, as it were, blotted out, and a fresh start was made.
Dispensationally, this may point to the period of man's
probation, from Adam's fall to the death of Christ.
Individually, it shows that at regeneration, the believer
ceases to be reckoned longer as a child of Adam, a fallen
sinner. He stands in Christ a new creation, he begins to
live in newness of life.   Old things are passed away : yea,
his former self is crucified and buried, and now bought *for*

* Appendix A.

God and born *of* God, he goes forth to live *for* God, no longer to serve sin, the world and Satan. Collectively, the Church as the body of Christ, and as a habitation of God "in the Spirit," came into existence after the Cross (Acts 2).

Apart from the death of Christ, and faith in Him who died, apart from the Person and work of Christ, there can be no real Christianity on earth, and no title to heaven hereafter. Redemption by blood, is the foundation of everything. The cross is the starting-point for the throne. The blood of the Lamb is the only title to the glory of God. And hence Jehovah commanded that the great redemption feast should be kept from year to year   (Exodus 13:10) throughout their generations. Immediately, they had crossed the threshold of their New Year, they were to celebrate the paschal feast. And this was to be continued even after they had reached the land of promise, and had been settled in their inheritance beyond Jordan. The memorial feast was still to be kept   (see Josh. 5:10 and Deut. 16),   and when generations to come should ask its meaning, they were to tell the story of their redemption (Exod. 12:24-27).

There are many precious details concerning the passover, over which we delight to meditate, which we need not now do more then mention. The choice of the lamb, its keeping up from the tenth to the fourteenth day, the manner and time of its death, and the use made of its blood, have their Antitypes in the Person and work of Christ.

It is worthy of our notice, that the aspect of the passover presented in this chapter, is not the same as we have in Exodus, chapter 12. There, the blood was sprinkled, and the flesh of the lamb roast with fire and eaten amid surrounding judgments. The cry of anguish was heard on every hand : it was the time of Divine judgment. They fed on the roasted lamb with girded loins, and shod feet, ready to depart. The passover was connected with their *salvation* and *separation* to God. But here it is "a feast of Jehovah," to be kept in the peace and rest of their Canaan inheritance, at the place where Jehovah chose to place His Name, while sweet savour offerings ascended from Jehovah's altar to His throne. It was Jehovah's feast, an expression of His own peculiar joy in the great event of which it was a shadow, and His redeemed people were gathered around Him to share that joy in His presence. What a wonderful thought is this! Jehovah keeping a feast in anticipation of the death of Christ! This passes our finite thought: we cannot comprehend it. What that death in all its fulness was to Him, no saint or angel can ever know. There were communications between Golgotha and the highest heaven, unknown and unknowable to man. That dying Sufferer was Jehovah's only son. That obedient, submissive Victim was the Lamb of God. That melted, tender heart, was the only heart on earth that ever and always beat true to God. Even in the hour of His darkest, deepest woe, He trusted in His God. " He became obedient unto death, even the death of the Cross," and that in a world where disobedience to God had reigned supreme. That perfect obedience unto death ; that complete surrender ; that unswerving devotion, was a " sweet savour " unto God. The Cross was a feast to Jehovah. It gave Him back more than sin had robbed Him of. Yes, blessed be God, there was that in the death of God's perfect, spotless Lamb which satisfied all His desires, and brought eternal salvation to all His people.

The Lord Jesus honoured the day of the passover by His death. He fulfilled the type in every detail. The lamb was killed in the evening (literally between the two

evenings, Exod. 12:6, margin), at the going down of the
sun (Deut. 16:6), as the one day was merging into the
other—for the Jewish day is reckoned from sunset to
sunset. Our blessed Lord observed the passover with His
disciples in the early hours of the fourteenth day, after
sunset ; it was night when Judas left the room.   The
remainder of that night was spent in Gethsemane. " Very
early " in the morning He was brought before the Council,
hurried from Caiaphas to Pilate, thence to Golgotha.
Darkness covered the land from the sixth till the ninth
hour, and at the ninth hour—three o'clock in the after-
noon—still on the fourteenth day, the Lamb of God died.

And thus the Scripture was fulfilled and the great
work accomplished which was to form the basis of all God's
dealings with man in grace and in judgment. The heavens
above will be filled with ransomed worshippers, each of
whom will own his only title there to the blood of the
Lamb, and own it in grateful song. Multitudes of the lost
in hell who have heard of, but despised the ransom provided, will be made to own and feel that the greatest of all
their sins, the fullest measure of their guilt on earth was, that
they rejected the Son of God, and despised His atoning
blood.

Feast of Unleavened Bread

" Seven days shalt thou eat unleavened bread therewith, even the bread of affliction " (Deut. 16:3).

" Let us keep the feast, not with old leaven, neither with the leaven of malice and wickedness. but with the unleavened bread of sincerity and truth " (1 Cor. 5:8, R.V.).

> *" Then within His home he led me,*
>   *Brought me where the feast is spread,*
> *Made me eat with Him my Father,*
>   *I, who begged for bondsman's bread.*
>
> *Not a suppliant at His gateway,*
>   *But a son within His home—*
> *To the love, the joy, the singing,*
>   *To the glory I am come."*

THE feast of unleavened bread began on the day after the Passover, and continued for seven days—a perfect period of time. The lamb was slain on the fourteenth day, at sunset ; the feast of unleavened bread began immediately after the fifteenth day commenced, which was just after sunset, so that there would be no lapse or loss of time and no interval between the death of the lamb, the sprinkling of the blood, and the keeping of the feast. And thus it was when the feast was first kept in the land of Egypt. The lamb was slain in the evening, the judgment fell at midnight, and the redeemed of the Lord were out of Egypt in the morning. The killing of the lamb was a single act, and the Passover was reckoned as a one-day feast, as was also the Feast of First-fruits,

Pentecost, and the Atonement. These one-day feasts all
point to certain great acts of Jehovah's hand, certain
definite transactions of His, perfect and complete in themselves, whereas those feasts which were of seven and
eight-day continuance, point to the outcome of these acts,
and their results in blessing to the people of God. Thus,
while the Passover is the type of Christ's death Godward,
the seven-day feast of unleavened bread, points to the whole
course and character of the believer's life on earth, from the
day of his conversion onward. It speaks of communion
with God based upon redemption, in holiness and truth.
The blood of Christ is the foundation of all true fellowship
with God : the Person of Christ,—feeding on the Lamb
slain—the only means whereby such fellowship may be
maintained ; and holiness—the putting away of leaven—
the condition necessary for its enjoyment. We have the
Holy Spirit's own exposition of this type fully given in
1 Cor. 5:7-8. R.V. —" Christ our passover is sacrificed for
us : wherefore let us keep the feast not with old leaven,
neither with the leaven of malice and wickedness ; but
with the unleavened bread of sincerity and truth ".*

The blood on the door-posts and lintel was the foundation of all ; not only of security, but of peace. There
could have been no peaceful feeding on the lamb, no
assurance of safety apart from it. No more can there be
true communion with God, until there is knowledge of
salvation and settled peace with God. This made secure,
then the lamb roast with fire, was placed on the table, and
around it the redeemed of the Lord gathered to keep the
feast. What a feast for the ransomed soul, is the Person of
Christ ! The Lamb of God sacrificed ! The Holy One of
God slain for sinners ! To feed on Him is strength. Girded

* Appendix B.

loins, shod feet, and staff in hand, all speak of pilgrimage.
They stood in Egypt, but they were not of it. They were
ready to go at the signal from heaven. So the saints of God
are but pilgrims here. The world is not their home. The
Cross has detached them from it, cut all the links that
bound them to it, and left them strangers here. As one
has sweetly sung—

> " The cords that bound my heart to earth
>   Were loosed by Jesus' hand ;
> Before His Cross I found myself
>   A stranger in the land."

The keeping of the feast in Egypt, in the wilderness, and in
Canaan, in the place where the Lord had placed His Name,
was always to be of the same character throughout. The
people's surroundings were different, but the feast remained
the same. Redemption as the basis of communion is unchangeable. Whether as " strangers " in the world ready
to depart, as in Exodus 12:2, or "pilgrims" in the
wilderness passing onward, as in Num. 9:1-3 or "possessors" of the land of promise, as in Josh. 5:10, the feast
was just the same. Thus we learn the saint's communion
is based on redemption, sustained by feeding on Christ,
and maintained in holiness and separation from evil.
These are principles of eternal value, unchangeable as the
character of God.

The feast was to be kept with " unleavened bread,"
and no leaven, or leavened bread was to be seen in their
habitations. It is worthy of notice, how strict and how
searching were the commandments of Jehovah concerning
leaven and its use. 1.—No leavened bread was to be
eaten. 2.—No leaven was to be seen. 3.—No leaven was
to be allowed in their houses (Exod. 13:7). The most
diligent search was required to be made in cup-board and

kneading-trough, to make sure that no atom of the corrupt thing was there, else " a little leaven " left and allowed, would soon leaven " the whole lump ".

Leaven is the figure of evil ; only evil, always evil, and of such evil as permeates and carries corruption with it wherever it works. There must be none of this allowed where communion with God is sought. Sin in the nature there always will be, but sin in practice, sin as it appears in its workings, there must not be, else communion with a holy God is impossible. " Put off the old man " : " Lay aside all malice " : " Put away lying," are words that show what God means by the putting away of leaven, by those who would commune with God. " Old leaven " may refer to old habits, old sins, and old associations, indulged and loved before conversion. These, especially in moments of unwatchfulness, are apt to assert their power, and seek to lead the believer into captivity. Well, it is, though humbling to remember, that the roots of every sin man was ever guilty of, remain in the flesh, and but for the restraining grace of God, and the indwelling Spirit, would yield their fruit. But if this be what is meant by " old leaven," what then can " new leaven " be ? May it not remind us that there are other forms of evil to which believers are subject, which, if they become unwatchful and neglectful of self-judgment, may mar their communion with God, as really as the grosser sins of their unregenerate days, if indulged, would surely do. Envy, jealousy, pride, boasting, conceit in spiritual things, a sectarian spirit, a desire to be uppermost, and a host of kindred sins, to which the unconverted are not exposed, Satan often uses in the circle of the fellowship of saints, for evil and corruption, in a way that he cannot use them in the world. These and all that leads up to them, must be judged and put away in

the saint, and in the assembly of saints, if communion with
God is to be maintained. Unleavened bread was to be
eaten seven days. " The unleavened bread of sincerity and
truth " is the Spirit's answer to this part of the type. Here
we have the positive side of the truth. The putting away
of leaven, is the negative side : eating " unleavened bread "
is the positive side, and it is well to remember and have
place for both. One-sided truth—either one or the other—
is dangerous, and when pressed beyond its measure is
disastrous. In the balance of truth, all sides duly pro-
portioned, is our safety. What is " sincerity " ? A " sin-
cere " man is usually taken to mean an earnest, well-
meaning person, who does what he believes to be right,
however far wrong his judgment may be. The word in
Phil. i. 10 means—" Pure when viewed in the sunlight".
Just as you would take a drop of water and hold it on your
finger between you and the sun. It is all clear : there is
no impurity in it. " Sincerity " implies that there has been
a holding of ourselves and our ways up to the light of God,
a continual judging of all our motives, ways, and works in
God's sunlight. No doubt this will often show what is not
" pure in the sunlight," and cause us to bow our heart in
confession, and our heads in shame before Him. Yet this
is His way, and it is the way of holiness and health to our
souls. It gives relish to the feast. Never does the soul so
enjoy Christ as when self-judged. Being in " the sunlight "
before God, leads always to the Cross and the Person of
Christ. "The bread of affliction" (Deut. 16:3), forms
part of the feast all the way through. " And *truth*." This
too forms part of the feast. The truth of God, His whole
counsel, must have its place ; no part kept back, no part
neglected, nothing exalted out of measure. Thus, " the
communion of saints "—a subject much spoken of but

little known—first with their God, and next with their brethren, will be sustained and continued through the " seven days " of earthly life, right on to that hour, when the resurrection morn shall break, and those on earth who wake and watch, together with all who sleep, will be introduced to the unbroken communion of the feast above, where the Lamb in the midst of the throne surrounded by hosts, who proclaim Him " Holy " and " Worthy," shall be still and ever the subject of their worship and the subject of their praise.

Feast of Firstfruits

" The first of the first-fruits *of thy land thou shalt bring into the house of the Lord thy God "* (Exod. 23:19).

" Now is Christ risen from the dead, and become the first-fruits *of them that slept "* (1 Cor. 15:20).

> *" First-fruits of the resurrection,*
> *He is risen from the tomb,*
> *Now I stand in new creation,*
> *Free, because beyond my doom."*

CLOSELY connected with the Passover, and while the feast of unleavened bread was in progress, the third of Jehovah's Feasts took place. This was the Feast of First-fruits. The land of Canaan was the proper scene of its celebration. Israel had observed the passover, and the feast of unleavened bread during the years of their pilgrimage in the wilderness (see Numb. 9:2-3), but before they could celebrate the Feast of First-fruits—or indeed any of the feasts that followed it—it was needful that they should be possessors of the Land of Promise.

Their calling and destiny was not the wilderness, but the land. They had indeed to pass through the wilderness, and learn its lessons (Deut. 8:3), but it was not to be their dwelling-place. The purpose of Jehovah, who had brought them out of Egypt by His out-streched arm of might, was to bring them into the goodly land flowing with milk and honey, " a land of wheat and barley, and vines, and fig-trees, and pomegranates " (Deut. 8:7-9), where they should lack nothing. Possessors of that land of fulness, this new ordinance of the sheaf of first-fruits was to have their care. In the midst of prosperity, the claims of Jehovah were to be first remembered. " Ye shall eat neither bread, nor parched corn, nor green ears, until the self-same day that ye have brought an offering unto your God." That offering was a sheaf reaped from the waving fields of ripened harvest, and carried to the priest, to be waved before the Lord to be accepted for them, followed by burnt-offering, meat-offering, and drink-offering—notably, no sin-offering. The time when this was to be done was, " the day after the Sabbath."

After the wilderness had been trodden, Jordan crossed, and Israel settled in the land of promise, they offered the sheaf of first-fruits, and reaped their harvests year after year. But they understood not the meaning of the ordinance. It was no more understood than was the killing of the paschal lamb, although both were foreshadowings of Christ. Another Lamb, another First-fruits, and other harvests, were in the mind of God. And when the full time had come for the great Antitype of these to be made known among men, they ought to have discerned and received Him with joy. But sin and unbelief had sealed their eyes. They saw no beauty in the Lamb of God when He was presented to them ; they led Him forth to the slaughter. Neither did they own and receive Him after He had as the First-fruits, risen from the dead, but forged a lie in face of His empty grave, and sought to stifle the voices of His servants, who preached His resurrection from among the dead. For this cause, Israel's harvests of blessing lie still unreaped, and the great Husbandman has gone forth to other fields, which—like as Samaria was in the days of the Lord's earthly ministry—are " white unto harvest " (John 4:35).

There can be no doubt that the sheaf of first-fruits reaped from the harvest field, on the morrow after the Sabbath, and waved before Jehovah in His temple for acceptance—the pledge to Israel of many sheaves to follow—was a type and foreshadowing of *Christ risen from the dead*. The very name of that sheaf, is the name given to Him as the One risen from among the dead—" Christ the First-fruits ". And then, as if to show the close connection of that sheaf with the harvest to follow, the Spirit adds—" Afterwards, they that are Christ's at His coming " (1 Cor. 15:23). The Lord Jesus honoured the day of the killing of the paschal lamb, by presenting Himself to God in death, " a Lamb without blemish and without spot ". He honoured the day of the waving of the sheaf of first-fruits, by presenting Himself to God as the First-born from among the dead. Israel's priest no doubt waved the sheaf in empty form, before a rent veil in the temple at Jerusalem, but outside the city's gates, God had reaped the Great Wave-sheaf from Joseph's tomb early that same morning. The Substance had come, and the shadow passed away. " When the Sabbath was past " (Mark 16:1), and the Marys had gone out " very early in the morning " to the tomb, they found it empty. The Lord had risen. The first great Sheaf had been reaped of that harvest, which God has since been gathering into the garners of heaven, all to be accepted in, and associated with their great Representative, the " First-born " from among the dead.

And here we might pause for a moment, and refresh our spirits, by a brief survey of this great gospel fact, the resurrection of Jesus Christ, and what it involves to Him, and to us. Even now the saints are " quickened together with Christ " (Eph. 2:5), they share His life, they are risen with Him (Col. 3:1). In incarnation, He was the *only-begotten* Son of God   (John 1:14; 3:16), and as such He stood alone. It has been erroneously taught, that in becoming man, He linked Himself with our race, and this raised men *as* men to a higher level.* But the Scriptures say not so. They clearly and definitely teach, that only by redemption and regeneration are sinners brought from death to life, and from Satan to God. This is the only way of vital union with Christ.

As " the corn of wheat " He stood alone, the only begotten of the Father; but having died, He arose, no longer alone, but as " the First-born from the dead " (Col. 1:18),   " the First-born among many brethren " (Rom. 8:29).). This new relation was first made known to Mary on the resurrection morning, in the ever-memorable words of the risen Christ in the garden—" I ascend to My Father and *your* Father, to my God and *your* God." And just as the acceptance of the sheaf of first-fruits presented before Jehovah was for the whole of Israel's harvest, so the acceptance and welcome to heaven given to Christ as the Representative of all His people, is the seal and the pledge of their welcome there. Yea, even now they stand in His acceptance; they are " accepted in the Beloved." The Father's love to Him is the measure of the Father's love to them (John 17:23). They are as near and dear to God as Christ is. Wonderful truth. Well may we sing—

> " So dear, so very dear to God,
>   More dear I cannot be ;
> The love wherewith He loves the Son,
>   Such is His love to me."

Such is the present sphere of blessing to which the resurrection of Christ introduces His people. And what about

* Appendix C.

the future ? Let us see. Resurrection of the dead (Heb. 6:2), is one of the great foundation truths of Scripture. It was denied by the Sadducees (Matt. 22:23), as it is now by modern Rationalists and " Higher Critics."* It was generally accepted among the Jews that there would be a " resurrection *of* the dead " (Acts 23:6). Martha of Bethany's words to the Lord concerning her brother Lazarus, aptly express the Jewish faith on the subject— " I know that he shall rise again in the resurrection at the last day " (John 11:24). This was all the light that had been given, but the Lord's answer in verse 25, tells of something brighter and better. Once and again he had hinted to His disciples that there would be a resurrection *from* (literally " from among the dead,"   Mark 9:9-10— see Newberry, Rotherham, etc.), but they did not grasp the meaning of His words. " Resurrection *of* the dead " is true of all; for all who have died, whether saved or lost, shall rise, though not at the same time, or for the same destiny. There will be a " resurrection of life " and a " resurrection of judgment " (John 5:29), a " resurrection of the just and the unjust " (Acts 24:15). The resurrection of the Lord Jesus was " from among the dead." and this is the word that is always used to describe the resurrection of His people. It will be an " out-resurrection" (Phil. 3:11, Newberry);   a resurrection "from among dead ones ". When the Lord shall descend from heaven with a shout—" the dead in Christ shall rise first " (1 Thess. 4:16). But the unconverted dead around them, will not stir on that fair morn. When the great First-fruit Sheaf was reaped, we read that " many bodies of the saints " that had fallen asleep were raised, and *after* His resurrection appeared (Matthew 27:15)—a pledge of

* Appendix D.

the greater harvest still to come—but not one sinner's tomb was stirred, not one of the unregenerate arose. So shall it be at the first resurrection. "The rest of the dead" live not again, until the thousand years of millennial blessedness have passed (Rev. 20:5), and then they are raised for judgment (Rev. 20:12). How vast the difference both in time and character is their resurrection from that of Christ and His saints !

The sweet-savour sacrifices which were offered on the same day as the sheaf was waved, may point to the ground of our association with, and acceptance in, the Risen Christ. He ascended to heaven in the excellency of His own peerless Person, but *our* title to be there with Him—now by faith, and soon in bodily presence—is found in the worth of the One Great Sacrifice offered *for* us. Even when we stand in resurrection bodies amid the glories of heaven, our song shall then as now be of the Lamb who was slain for us.

> " I stand upon His merit,
>   I know no other stand ;
> Not e'en where glory dwelleth—
>   In Immanuel's land."

Pentecost, the Feast of Weeks

*" Thou shalt keep the feast of weeks unto the Lord thy God,
with a tribute of a free-will offering of thine hand, which thou shalt
give unto the Lord thy God "* (Deut. 16:10).

*" When the day of Pentecost was being fulfilled, they were all
together in one place "* (Acts 2:1).

" Ye are all one in Christ Jesus " (Gal. 3:28).

*" O teach us, Lord, to know and own
This wondrous mystery ;
That Thou with us art truly one,
And we are one with Thee."*

FIFTY days after the wave-sheaf had been reaped and
presented, the redeemed people were again gathered
to the place where Jehovah had placed His Name.
This was to celebrate the Feast of Weeks, or Pentecost.
The former of these names is derived from the fact, that
the celebration of this feast was seven weeks or a week of
weeks after the First-fruits. The latter name, " Pentecost."
describes the same period by days, the Greek word
" pentecoste " meaning—the fiftieth. The services of the
Feast of Weeks consisted in a new meat-offering being
offered before the Lord. This meat-offering was to be
two loaves of fine flour—fruit of the new harvest which
had just been gathered in—baked " with leaven," then
waved by the priest, accompanied by sweet savour and sin
offerings. There is a striking similarity, and a close con-

nection between this feast and the First-fruits. They are introduced in Lev. 23:9 by the usual introductory words—" And tne Lord spake unto Moses, saying," and these words do not again occur till verse 23, where the Feast of Trumpets is introduced. Thus, as the Passover, and the Feast of Unleavened Bread are associated together, so are the Feast of First-fruits and Pentecost.

We have already seen that the answer to the Passover has been found in the death of Christ, and that the First-fruits has had its fulfilment in His resurrection from among the dead. We have now to inquire whether there has been a fulfilment of Pentecost, and if so, what that fulfilment is. The antitype of this feast is found in the descent of the Holy Spirit, and the formation of the saints into " one new man," composed of believing Jews and Gentiles. Just as our Lord honoured the day of the Passover by His death, and as God the Father honoured the day of the First-fruits, by raising up Christ from among the dead, as the First-fruits of a glorious harvest so the Holy Spirit honoured the feast of Pentecost by His descent upon the waiting and expectant disciples, who, when that day was " being ful-filled " (Acts 2:1, R.V.), were found gathered together waiting for the promised Comforter. On these waiting souls the Spirit descended, uniting them into one body (1 Cor. 12:13) filling each one, and filling the whole house in which they were assembled. This was the inaug-uration of a new work of God's grace among the sons of men, such as had not been seen in ages that had gone before. What are the special characteristics of this work ? Let us turn to our type, and examining its various parts in the light of New Testament Scripture we shall see.

The First-fruits pointed to the Risen Christ accepted for His people within the heavens. The loaves of Pentecost

are also called " first-fruits unto the Lord "   (Lev. 23:17).
This identifies them with the wave-sheaf.   It was the pre-
cursor of the harvest.   The loaves were made of flour, from
the same crop as that sheaf.   They were of the same grain,
reaped from the same field, only the wave-sheaf was in all
things pre-eminent.   So it is with Christ and His believing
people.   He is " the First-fruits "   (1 Cor. 15:20).   And of
the saints it is written—" Of His own will begat He us
with the Word of Truth, that we should be a kind of
first-fruits of His creatures " (James 1:18).   He is the
" First-born," they are " His brethren "   (Rom. 8:29);
all of one (Heb. 2:11);   "the Church of the first-born "
(Heb. 12:23).   Glorious truth ! Let it be received into the
heart in all its unction and blessing.   What a power it
brings with it to the soul ! What a horizon it opens to the
spiritual vision ! One with Christ ! Standing before God
in Christ, accepted, complete, filled full.   No more in
fallen Adam of the earth; but in the Second Man, the last
Adam, Christ risen and ascended to Heaven.   This is the
place of every believer; God has given it to all His people.
How few believe it, and how little do any of us enjoy it !
Yet there it is, given us by our God to be apprehended,
received, and enjoyed from day to day.   How is this to be ?
By the indwelling Spirit, given to each believer.   He is a
witness of the exaltation of Christ (Heb. 10:15; Acts 2:
32:34).   "The *first-fruits* of the Spirit" (Rom 8:23),
given to all believers, is the seal of their oneness with
Christ (Eph. 1:13), the earnest and pledge of their resurrection, and association with Him in glory, and the power
for enjoyment of this great truth.   Apart from Christ's
glorification at God's right hand, the Spirit would not have
come down to indwell believers (John 16:7).   His presence
in, and with them, is the witness that Christ is accepted at

the right hand of God (John 15:26). The presence of the
Holy Spirit on earth, and the union of believers with the
Risen Christ at God's right hand by the Spirit, are the two
great characteristics of this present age.

The two loaves point to the fact that God is gathering
out from Jew and Gentile, a people for Himself. Before
Pentecost, these two peoples were divided by a " middle
wall." The Jews were the chosen seed. To them pertained
" the adoption, and the glory, and the covenants " (Rom.
9:14). " Unto them were committed the oracles of God "
(Rom. 3:2); whereas the Gentiles were aliens and strangers, afar off, and without God (Eph. 2:12). Both had
shewn themselves against Christ, and in that memorable
prayer offered to God, when opposition to God's grace
had been shewn in Jerusalem, these words were uttered—
" Against thy holy Servant Jesus, Whom Thou didst
anoint, both Herod and Pontius Pilate, with the *Gentiles*,
and the *peoples of Israel* were gathered together " (Acts 4:
27, R.V.). God had concluded there was " no difference "
(Rom. 3:22). The Cross had manifested their common
guilt, and hatred of Christ. It had also broken down the
middle wall of partition that divided them. Now, by the
descent of the Holy Spirit, the twain—that is, believing
Jews and believing Gentiles—were formed into " one new
man " (Eph. 2:15). The Cross reconciled *both* in one
body to God, and in one Spirit *both* have access to the
Father (Eph. 2:16-18, R.V.). This great work was inagur-
ated by the descent of the Spirit on the day of Pentecost,
and here is beautifully set forth in type, by the two wave-
loaves being presented together as one before the Lord.
This was the mystery " hid in God," which had not been
made known in former ages—" that the Gentiles are
fellow-heirs, and fellow-members of the body, and fellow-

partakers of the promise in Christ Jesus " (Eph. 3:6, R.V.), and that it is written, " in one Spirit were we all baptised into one body, whether Jews or Greeks, whether bond or free, and were all made to drink of one Spirit (1 Cor. 12: 13, R.V.). This is the unique and privileged place given to the saints of this age, to all saints of every clime, from Pentecost till the advent of the Lord to the air, to call His people away from earth to heaven. It is the special calling and portion of the church, the body of Christ, in contrast to all which had gone before, and that will follow after. It might be summed up thus—Union With Christ the Head in heaven, and with all His saints by the Holy Spirit. Truly, " this is the Lord's doing, and it is marvellous in our eyes ". And let it be remembered, that being the workmanship of God, the Church thus formed, is indissolubly and eternally one. Men can neither mar nor mutilate it. Its unity is Divinely created and Divinely sustained, so that against it, the gates of hell shall never prevail. Such is the Church viewed in its heavenly and Divine relationship to Christ, begun at Pentecost by the descent of the Spirit, now being gathered and fashioned by the Lord, and which, when completed, will be raised, and presented in all the perfectness of Christ to God.

The two wave-loaves point also to the Church in another aspect, namely : that which is earthly and visible, as it first appeared on that same Pentecost-day and the days that followed. On that day, there was brought into existence, a united company of believers, of one heart and soul, found together, and manifesting before men their common interests in Christ, and in each other—a heavenly people in mortal flesh on earth, indwelt by the heaven-sent Spirit, manifesting His fruits, and standing forth in His power before the eyes of men. It was to this company that

the name of "the Church" (Acts 5:11; 8:1) was first
given. It was chiefly, or wholly composed of believing
Jews at first, but in process of time the Gospel reached
unto the Gentiles through Peter's lips—who had been
chosen as the instrument to open the door of faith to the
Jews first, and afterwards to the Gentiles (see Matt. 16:18;
Acts 2:14, with 15:7). Others were brought into this
" one flock " (John 10:16), and thus believing Gentiles
became manifestly associated with believing Jews, and
together formed the " Churches of God in Jesus Christ "
(1 Thess. 2:14) wherever found. This, although at first
slowly owned by believing Jews, and even by Peter himself
(Acts 10:28; 11:3-18) was the earthly answer to the heavenly
pattern, and was afterwards more fully made known *to* and
by the apostle Paul, " the wise master-builder " (1 Cor. 3:
10), to whom, by revelation, the full pattern of the Church's
constitution, fellowship, ordinances, ministry, and rule
was committed, and who, in his epistles, has passed the
same on to us, and to all saints of this age (see 1 Cor. 11-
14; 1 Tim 3:1-16). This divine legislation for the
Church as given in the Word, continues through the entire
age, and God has neither repealed nor added to it since it
was given. Happy had it been for saints, had they received
and acted on it, apart from the traditions and commandments of men.

The two wave-loaves were baked " with leaven ".
Leaven is everywhere and always the type of corruption.
There was no leaven in the meat-offering (Lev. 2:11),
because that offering is a type of the perfect manhood and
character of Christ. He was intrinsically holy in His
character and ways. Not so with His people. Even after
conversion, and with the Spirit indwelling, the believer is
not personally free from corruption. The flesh still dwell s

within him : the presence of the Spirit does not expel or
alter it, although by grace its power is no longer dominant.
It is restrained, but not eradicated, hence the believer is
not sinless.   He is not as was Jesus Christ his Lord, fit to
be placed on the altar for Divine acceptance, for atoning
and meritorious sacrifice.   Hence we read with, or
over the wave-loaves, sin-offering and sweet-savour offerings were presented for their acceptance.   The two loaves
were thus presented to Jehovah, with leaven *in* them, but
under the shelter and covered with the preciousness of
these offerings.   And thus it is, that believers individually,
and the Church collectively, stand as a new meat-offering
before God, accepted in all the value of Christ's peerless
Person, and atoning work.   The moment that either
individual Christians, or God's Churches on earth, suppose
that personal devotion or service, or that any measure of
obedience to the truth give title before God, or that gifts
and graces eradicate the corruption that dwells within,
they will find out sooner or later that they have been the
subject's of Satan's deception.   The Church in its early
beauty and freshness had within its bosom the leaven, and
soon in varied aspects, it began to manifest itself, both in
doctrine and practice.   It was found in the Church at
Jerusalem (Acts 5:1; 15:1), the Churches at Galatia
(Gal. 5:9), and the Church of God at Corinth (1 Cor. 5:
6-7).   And in these last days when new and unheard of
departures from the faith are continually being multiplied,
when doctrines of demons pour forth on every hand, and
when evil men and seducers wax worse and worse, the
appearance of leaven in its various forms, need not alarm,
although it should always humble the saints of God, and
send them to seek anew the repose of their souls individually
and the only foundation on which they stand, collectively

as God's Church, sanctified in Christ Jesus   (1 Cor. 1:2),
to be the Spirit's holy temple (1 Cor. 3:17) in the peerless
Person, and ever-precious Work of Christ.

> " His precious blood is all my plea,
>   My only title there ;
> Hmself my costly offering,
>   Unblemished pure and rare."

The Present Interval

" God did visit the Gentiles to take out of them a people for His Name " (Acts 15:14).

" Blindness in part is happened to Israel, until the fulness of the Gentiles be come in " (Rom. 11:25).

> *" His chosen Bride, ordained with Him,*
> *To reign o'er all the earth ;*
> *Must first be formed, ere Israel know*
> *Her Saviour's matchless worth."*

A LONG period of full four months intervened between the Feast of Weeks and the Feast of Trumpets, during which the harvest and the vintage were gathered in. There was no holy convocation of the people during these busy months. No fresh subject of interest was introduced to occupy their thoughts, save the reaping of the fruits of that goodly land on which Jehovah's eye and heart were ever resting. The answer to this is found in the work of God throughout this present age. Since the day of Pentecost, on which the Spirit of God descended, and the gathering out of a people from all nations to form the Church, the body of Christ began there has no new operation of God's hand been put forth among men. The work of proclaiming the Gospel among, and the discipling men of all nations (Matt. 28:19), has been going on ever since. The dispensation then inaugurated, continues still, and that mystic body, of which all the members were written in God's book (Psa. 139:16) before the foundation of the world (Eph. 1:4), is still in continuance being fashioned, under the hand of the Spirit. And this work will continue until the advent of the Son of God from heaven. The dispensation that now runs its course, began at the descent of the Spirit, and will end at the descent of the Son, and the ascent of the saints to heaven. This simple fact remembered, will keep the saints of God from being led into bye-paths of error, as to present fulfilments of prophecy regarding the earthly people, and the application of Scriptures to the events of the present period, which can only have their fulfilment in a coming age, after the call of the Church is complete.*

As regards Israel, they are at present broken off, " until the fulness of the Gentiles " has been gathered in (Rom. 11:25). No prophecy concerning their full restoration and future glory, can possibly be fulfilled while the present dispensation runs its course, but after the call and ingathering of the Church has been completed, God will turn His heart and hand to His earthly people. And then " times and seasons " (Acts 1:7) and the threads of God's promise and prophecy towards His earthly people, will be taken up again just where they were broken off. Then prophetic dates will again resume their course. During the present age, believing Jews are incorporated in the church, the body of Christ, but they are as few in number as the " gleanings of the corners of the harvest-field " (Lev. 23), a feeble " remnant according to the election of grace " (Rom. 11:5). When the Lord puts forth His hand to recover and re-gather His earthly people as a nation, it will be by other agencies than the gospel as now

* Appendix E.

preached among the nations, and with more wide-spread results.

There is no indication here, or elsewhere in Scripture, that the present dispensation will run its course until the end of time, or that the world will be converted by the Gospel as now proclaimed among the sons of men. The Lord will accomplish His purpose in the gathering of His earthly people and the subjugation of the world to its rightful King by other means. What these are, the remaining feasts of this prophetic chapter will show.

And here, it may be well to notice, that the remaining feasts—which all took place in the seventh month, and followed each other in quick succession, have a double meaning. They have a heavenly and an earthly fulfilment, that is, their antitypes and answers will be found in events yet to take place in the heavens and in the earth as recorded in the Word. In days to come, the operations of the Divine hand toward those who share the heavenly calling and belong to heaven, and likewise toward His earthly people, who in days to come will again be in covenant relationship with Jehovah, will proceed simultaneously. The heavens and the earth will not then, as now, be separated by sin, but united in one, for "in that day there shall be one Lord and His Name one " (Zech. 14:9), and unto Him shall the gathering of the people be. The same glorified Lord will be the Head of the Church, the King of Israel and the Lord of Creation. He will be honoured by all in the heavens above, and in the earth beneath, and men of every nation, people, and tongue, will unite to own Jesus of Nazareth " Lord of all."

> " To Thee the world her treasure brings,
>   To Thee the mighty bow ;
> To Thee the Church exulting springs,
>   Her Sovereign-Saviour Thou."

Feast of Trumpets

" *The* trumpet *shall sound ; and the dead shall be raised incorruptible, and we shall be changed* " *(1 Cor. 15:52).*

" *He shall send His angels with a great sound of a* trumpet, *and they shall gather together His elect* " *(Matt. 24:31).*

> " *Hark to the trump ! behold it breaks*
> *The sleep of ages now,*
> *And lo ! the light of glory shines*
> *On many an aching brow.*"
>
> .   .   .   .   .
>
> " *The scattered sons of Israel's race,*
> *That Trumpet's sound shall bring*
> *Back to their land : to know and own*
> *Messiah as their King.*"

THE Feast of Trumpets, which was observed on the first day of the seventh month, begins the second series of " Jehovah's set feasts," and it was quickly followed by the Day of Atonement, and the Feast of Tabernacles. As has been already indicated, these remaining feasts all point forward to great events of the future, which God will yet bring to pass, both for His heavenly and His earthly people, for in the days that are to come, He will glorify and exalt His Christ in the heavens above, and in the earth beneath, and gather together in one under Him, things celestial and things terrestrial (Eph. 1:10).

The blowing of trumpets was an ancient ordinance in Israel. In their wilderness days, two silver trumpets

(Num. 10:2), made of the atonement money of the people, were blown " for the calling of the assembly, and for the journeyings of the camps ". In days of gladness, and in times of war, the blast of the trumpet was a familiar sound among the thousands of Israel. It was the voice of Jehovah their Redeemer, who had brought them out from Egypt to be unto Himself a special people. All his command-ments were given on the ground of redemption, and as His redeemed people, He claimed their obedience. The application of this to the saints of this time is plain enough. The Lord's people are a purchased people, " a people for His own possession " (Titus 2:14, R.V.),   redeemed from all lawlessness; no longer their own, but bought with a price to glorify God (1 Cor. 6:20), and as obedient children to do His will.

His commandments are not grievous; they fall on the ear of His people as the words of their Redeemer, and constrained by love to Him, they swiftly obey. It was of such obedience that the Psalmist sang—" Blessed is the people that knew the *trumpet sound*, they walk O Lord, in the light of Thy countenance " (Psa. 89:15, R.V.).
And thus it is that communion with God is sustained, by loving, loyal, hearty, uncompromising obedience to every word that comes to us from Him who has redeemed us. This even now, in the wilderness days of the saints, is unto God as a feast, which as in days of old He comes to share (Gen. 18:1-18) with His obedient people (John 14:23) and they with Him (Rev. 3:20). But the full answer to the Feast of Trumpets is yet to come, and will have its grand fulfilment in that coming day when " The Lord Himself shall descend from heaven with a shout, with the voice of the archangel and with the trump of God " (1 Thess. 4:16). When at "the last trump" (1 Cor. 15:

52) the dead in Christ shall be raised incorruptible, having
put on incorruptibility, and the living changed, having put
on immortality, both will together ascend to meet their
Lord in the air.

> " Him eye to eye we then shall see,
>   Our face like His shall shine ;
> O what a glorious company
>   When saints and angels join."

With what joy and triumph the sons of Israel in ancient
days gathered to the city of the Great King, as the silvery
blast of the trumpet rang out through all their land ! But
what will it be, when " the last trump " shall sound, and
the whole of the redeemed shall rise to meet their Lord ?
Who can describe or conceive the bliss of that moment ?
What a triumph over death ! The grave swept of all the
ransomed dead ! The world cleared of all the living saints,
and all gathered in resurrection beauty to their home above.

> " Ascending through the crowded air,
>   On eagle wings they soar
> To dwell in the full joy of love,
>   And sorrow there no more."

And this feast of Trumpets will have its fulfilment in the
awakening and gathering of God's earthly people Israel.
Long have they been as in the slumber of death, a people
scattered and peeled, but the " set time " to favour Zion
(Psa. 102:13) will come. The prophetic Scriptures of the
Old Testament teem with glowing words descriptive of
this event, when the trumpet shall be blown in Zion
(Psa. 81:3), and the long-lost and scattered people shall
flock around their once-rejected Lord and King. It was
of this that the Lord Himself spake on that day, looking
far onward to the time of the end, after He had wept over

Jerusalem, which then refused to be gathered under His
sheltering wing. He told them they should " see the Son
of Man coming in the clouds of heaven, with power and
great glory. And He shall send His angels with a sound of
a great trumpet, and they shall gather His elect from the
four winds, from the one end of heaven to the other "
(Matt. 24:30, 31). This refers to the earthly people
being gathered to their land, at the coming of the Son of
Man to earth, whereas the heavenly people are to be
gathered around Him, when, at an earlier period He
descends to the air as Son of God. In the heavens above,
they see His face without a veil, and bask in the light of
His countenance. The "outcasts of Israel and the dis-
persed of Judah," the earthly people, as those " ready to
perish" (Isa. 27:13), will be gathered* one by one from
distant lands and isles to Immanuel's land. These events
will be unto God and His Christ, occasions of deepest joy,
which even now prospectively He shares with His ransomed
people.

> " O Zion, when thy Saviour came,
>   In grace and love to thee ;
> No beauty in thy royal Lord,
>   Thy faithless eye could see.
>
> Yet onward in His path of grace,
>   The holy Sufferer went,
> To feel at last that love on thee,
>   Had all in vain been spent.
>
> Yet not in vain—o'er Israel's land
>   The glory yet will shine ;
> And He, thy once-rejected King,
>   For ever shall be thine."

* This gathering—foretold by the dying patriarch (Genesis 49:
10), must not be confused with an earlier return of part of the
covenant people to their land in unbelief, when they will enter
into a compact with Antichrist only to be deceived (see Daniel
9:27).

Day of Atonement

" *On that day shall the priest make an atonement for you, to cleanse you, that ye may be clean from all your sins before the Lord* " (Lev. 16:30).

" *So Christ also having been once offered to bear the sins of many, shall appear a second time, apart from sin, to them that wait for Him unto salvation* " (Heb. 9:28, R.V.).

" *There in righteousness transcendent,*
 Lo ! He doth in Heaven appear ;
Shews the Blood of His atonement,
 As thy title to be there."

THE Day of Atonement, was Israel's annual cleansing from sin. A full account of all the services of this eventful day will be found in Leviticus, chap. 16, as given by Jehovah through Moses to Aaron. Here, in Lev. 23, as in the other feasts, it is viewed especially from the Divine side, as a feast of Jehovah, expressive of the joy derived by Him from the atoning death of Christ.

It is worthy of notice, that the day on which the blood was carried within the veil and sprinkled there before and on the mercy-seat, was the tenth day of the seventh month. The seventh month had been changed to the first month, at the time of Israel's deliverance from Egypt. The paschal lamb was henceforth to be chosen from the flock, and set apart for sacrifice on the tenth day of this month. Its death on the fourteenth day was the foundation of all that followed, as we gather from the facts that the Feast

of Unleavened Bread, the First-fruits, and the Feast of
Weeks, are all dated from the Passover. The seventh
month begins the second half of Israel's year, and the
second series of Jehovah's set feasts. And here again on
the tenth day of that month the blood of a victim is the
prominent feature, but not to be used as in the Passover.
There, the blood of the lamb was sprinkled on the lintel
and side-posts of the door, to avert the stroke of judgment
on Israel's first-born sons. Here the blood is carried
within the veil and put on the mercy-seat. In the former
case it is the sacrifice of Christ, appropriated by faith, as
that which alone can deliver the sinner from righteous
wrath, but in this ordinance, it is the blood of atonement
presented Godward as that by which His throne is established in righteousness, His claims fully met, the believer
permitted to draw near in spirit now to commune with God,
and the ground on which he will enter the presence of
God in person by and by. The sacrifices of the Day of
Atonement were—1. A sin-offering and a burnt-offering
for Aaron and his house. 2. Two goats for a sin-offering
and a ram for a burnt-offering for the congregation.

The blood of the sin-offering for Aaron and his house
was sprinked on the mercy-seat once, and before it seven
times, and over the sprinkled blood a cloud of sweet
incense, covered the mercy seat. The word " atonement "*—which occurs no less than forty-eight times in
the Book of Leviticus alone— means " a covering." The
blood covered the mercy-seat, so also did the *cloud* of
incense, and in this we have an exceedingly expressive
type of the *work* and *worth* of the Lord Jesus Christ, in
whose blood the believer is made nigh to God, and in
whose Person he stands accepted. The atoning blood

* Appendix F.

covers all his sin. The perfectness of Christ encircles his person. The " house " of Aaron stood in the same accept-ance as Aaron himself, and thus " the household of faith," the priestly house of New Testament times, composed of all true believers (1 Peter 2:5), has access even *now* into the holiest of all (Heb. 10:19), and are made meet to be partakers of the inheritance of the saints in light (Col. 1: 12). The blood of the goat for the congregation upon which the Lord's lot fell, was likewise sprinkled within the veil, and then the sins of the people were confessed by Aaron over, and put upon the head of the scapegoat. It was then sent away into the wilderness. Thus the claims of Jehovah were all met, the priesthood was established, and the congregation cleansed from all their sins before the Lord, and set at rest. The answer to all this, in so far as it applies to the saint of this time, is fully given in the Epistles of the New Testament, where the cleansing (Heb. 10:17-18), the acceptance (Eph. 1:6), and the access (Heb. 10:19; 4:16) of believers is made fully known. But the aspect of the truth here set forth, has special reference to the future. The Day of Atonement—in its order—comes after the Feast of Trumpets, and before the Feast of Tabernacles. We have already seen that the answer to the Feast of Trumpets, in its application to the heavenly people will be, the coming of the Lord Jesus as Son of God from heaven; and to the earthly people, His coming as Son of Man to earth. The Feast of Tabernacles—as we shall see presently—looks forward to the millennial reign of Christ. The Day of Atonement comes in between. To what event then does it point ? Where are we to find its antitype ? Clearly, it must be something after the Advent of the Lord, and before His Kingly reign. Its answer in respect of the heavenly people, is their reception to the immediate presence of God as priests, their establishment around His throne to sing redemption's song (Rev. chaps. 4-5),   and as the servants of Jesus Christ, in their manifestion before His judgment-seat, to have their service reviewed, and their work rewarded   (2 Cor. 5:10; Rev. 22:12).   In that full blaze of heavenly light to which the redeemed shall be introduced in the highest heaven, the immediate dwelling-place of God, the value of the blood of Christ will be known by them as it never was before. So also will the exceeding sinfulness of sin, the marvellous grace of God, and the fulness of Christ's redemption. There, amid holy and heavenly hosts, surrounding God's throne, the slain Lamb in the midst, will still be the object of their worship, and the theme of their song.   The eye of God will rest with ineffable delight on that glorified throng, each member of which stands *on* the merit of the blood of the Lamb, and encircled with His excellence

This will be a rich feast of Jehovah, and the saints themselves will share it, each and all.

> " God's eye of flame that searches all,
>   And finds e'en heaven unclean,
> Rests on each soul in full delight,
>   For not a spot is seen :
> Cleansed every whit in Jesus' blood,
>   Whate'er its guilt has been."

The manifestion of the risen saints before the judgment seat of Christ, will be a further answer to this type.   At this tribunal, not their salvation, or the acceptance of their persons, but the character of their service will be under review.   The hidden motives, the manifestation of the secrets of all hearts will be there shewn in the light of heaven, and to the saints themselves.   Then shall they know, even as they are known.   The failures of the path,

the imperfections of what once seemed so pure and perfect,
will be seen as they had never been seen before, and the
Master's estimate of all, will be known. What a change
from present estimates of service that hour will bring!
How small will that which often bulks in men's opinions
and obtains their praise, appear then! How great those
little acts and hidden deeds known only now to Christ and
to God.

> " Deeds of merit as we thought them,
>   He will shew us were but sin ;
> Little acts we had forgotten,
>   He will own were done for Him."

But while there will be much to humble the saints at
Christ's judgment-seat, there will be nothing to condemn
them, for the blood of atonement, the memorial of the
ever-precious death of the Lamb of God, will speak forth
its value, and cover all the sins and failures of the Lord's
redeemed. Then after all has been manifested—the good
rewarded, the bad burnt up—the saints and servants of
God will pass into their places in the kingdom of their
Lord, in the perfect enjoyment of rest. And thus the three
features of the Day of Atonement—acceptance, humilia-
tions, and rest—will be fulfilled in the risen saints. How
all this will enhance the value of the blood of the Lamb!*
And if—as has been suggested by another—the devil,
the accuser of the brethren, will not at this time have been
cast from the heavens, as he will be at a later period (Rev.
12:10-11), but will seek to accuse the saints before God,
on account of the failures of their service as made known
at Christ's judgment-seat, He will be answered in this,

* Appendix G.

His last attempt to dispute their title to heaven, by the atoning death of Christ. As it is written, " they overcame him by the blood of the Lamb ".

The fulfilment of the type in regard to the earthly people is fully and touchingly described in the prophetic Scriptures. Delivered from the allied forces of Antichrist, and his confederate kings, who at that moment will surround the earthly Jerusalem, by the sudden appearance of the Lord on Mount Olivet, they will look up to find that He, who is their great Deliverer, is Jesus of Nazareth, whom they crucified. The wounded hands and feet, will bring back to mind and conscience, that hour, when in their hatred of Him, they cried out—" Crucify Him ", and made the awful request—" His blood be upon us, and upon our children ". Now they look on Him, whom they pierced and mourn. And what a mourning that will be, when " the Spirit of grace, and of supplication " is poured out upon them, and their melted hearts are turned to the Lord. Their bitterness and grief passes all description, as they look upon Him whom they had crucified and slain. The deep searchings of heart of Joseph's brethren, as they remembered their cruelty to him, are but a faint illustration of the anguish of awakened Israel in the latter day, when every household, and individual apart, alone before God will mourn, as one mourneth for an only son, their rejection of the Messiah. But just as when the anguish of Joseph's brethren was at its depth, the vail that hid him as their brother was removed, and he in grace revealed himself to them as their kinsman and deliverer, so will the glorified Christ reveal Himself, and His atoning work, to the melted hearts of awakened Israel, and they will turn to find the repose of their souls in the atoning death of the Lamb slain. Then it will be, that the language of Isaiah liii. will burst from their lips—" Surely He hath borne our griefs, and carried our sorrows; yet we did esteem Him stricken, smitten of God, and afflicted. But He was wounded for our transgressions, He was bruised for our iniquities."* And in that bruising their healing will be found, for " in that day there shall be a fountain opened to the house of David, and to the inhabitants of Jerusalem, for sin, and for separation and uncleanness " (Zech. 13:1). margin). Not a new sacrifice, but the abiding efficacy of the one Great Sacrifice of Calvary extended to them. Thus humbled, cleansed from sin, and brought to God, they will pass into the millennial kingdom, under the benign rule of the Prince of Peace with His heavenly bride.

> " Then thou, beneath the peaceful reign
>   Of Jesus and His bride,
>   Shalt sound His grace and glory forth,
>   To all the earth beside.
>
>   The nations to thy glorious light,
>   O Zion, yet shall throng ;
>   And all the listening islands wait
>   To catch the joyful song.
>
>   The Name of Jesus yet shall ring
>   Through earth and heaven above,
>   And all His ransomed people know
>   The Sabbath of His love."

* Appendix H.

Feast of Tabernacles

" The feast of ingathering, which is in the end of the year, when thou hast gathered in thy labours out of the field " (Exod. 23:16).

" Hereafter ye shall see heaven opened, and the angels of God ascending and descending upon the Son of Man " (John 1:51).

*" Then the heavens, the earth, and the sea shall rejoice,
The field and the forest shall lift the glad voice,
The sands of the desert shall flourish in green,
And Lebanon's glory be shed o'er the scene."*

THE Feast of Tabernacles was the last of Jehovah's feasts, a season of great joy and rejoicing, a kind of harvest-home, after the harvest and the vintage had been gathered in. Its eighth day, is said to be the " closing festival " (Lev. 23:36, R.V. margin), the last great scene of Jehovah's joy in the accomplishment of His purposes of grace, in which His gathered people are permitted to share.

The antitype of the Feast of Tabernacles, like those of the two that preceded it—is still in the future. Nothing that has yet taken place, answers to this season of festive joy; its answer is to be found in the future day of glory, when Christ and His risen saints shall fill the heavens above, reigning over a restored and rejoicing world; when Israel, restored to their long-lost land, and owning Jesus of Nazareth their Lord and King, shall be the first of the nations, and when, under the peaceful beams of the Sun

of Righteousness, the groaning creation shall rejoice and
be glad.

The feast was kept for eight days, after the corn and
the wine had been gathered in. " Thou shalt observe the
Feast of Tabernacles seven days, after thou hast gathered
in thy corn and wine " (Deut. 16:13). This enables us
to see exactly where its antitype comes in, in the dispensa-
tional dealings of God. Israel's harvest consisted of two
parts—the corn and the wine. The " corn of wheat "
(John 12:24), which fell into the ground and died, but
rose again with others associated with it, having the same
nature and proceeding from its stem, represents Christ
risen from the dead, with all His heavenly people. The
ingathering of the harvest has its answer in the whole of
the heavenly people, all who share in the first resurrection,
being gathered safely home to the garners of heaven. The
vintage of the earth (Rev. 14:18-19), and the treading of
the winepress of God's wrath, has reference to the gathering
of Christ's enemies for judgment. After these events
have taken place, then the millennial reign of Christ will
begin. In common with the two preceding feasts, the
Feast of Tabernacles has an application to the heavenly,
and also to the earthly people, although here, the dividing
line between the celestial and the terrestrial, between
things in heaven and things on earth, is not so sharp as in
the answers to the previous types, simply because in that
coming day of Immanuels's reign, the heavens and the
earth will not be as they now are, sundered and ruled by
opposing forces. For in the day of " the restitution of all
things," heaven and earth, and all that in them is, will
own Jesus Christ as Lord of all.* To the raised and heavenly

* Appendix I.

saints, it speaks of the joy and honour they shall share with their Lord, when, in manifested glory they shall appear as the Bride, the Lamb's wife, to reign for ever with Him.

> "He and I in that bright glory
> One deep joy shall share;
> Mine to be for ever with Him,
> His that I am there."

To the earthly people, the Feast of Tabernacles points to the joy and rejoicing that awaits them in the latter days. This feast will then be kept, and all nations will go up to the city of the Great King to celebrate it (Zech. 14:16, 17).

"Booths made of palm trees and willows of the brook," reminded them of wilderness days. The palm, in remembrance of victories won by His grace, the willow in memory of the tears wiped away by His hand. Surely, even amid the glories of heaven, the saints will remember these, and their memory will send forth in gushing streams of praise to God and the Lamb, the homage of their hearts, as they own the rule of Him, who sits upon the throne. To the earthly people the palm bespeaks their share in the triumph and glory of Christ. But in the midst of that scene of triumphant joy, can Judah fail to remember, that in days gone by, the Victor's royal brow was once in these very scenes rudely wreathed with thorns by her hand, and that there, where now the beams of glory shine, stood once the shameful Cross of Golgotha, on which her Crucified Messiah hung. The memorial sacrifices which they then shall offer on Jehovah's altar, like the "willows of the brook," will be the memorials of the sorrows and the sacrifice of the Lamb of God. As we sing now of that coming day—

"Ye saints whose love can ne'er forget
The wormwood and the gall;
Go spread your trophies at His feet,
And crown Him Lord of all."

The transfiguration scene, on "the holy mount," unveils
to us more fully the millennial kingdom it its various
parts. The Lord told His disciples before He led them
up to be "apart" that they would "see the kingdom of
God" (Luke 9:27), and Peter speaks of the transfiguration as "the *power* and *coming* of our Lord Jesus Christ"
(2 Peter 1:16). In "the excellent glory," high above all,
on His throne, was God, whose voice was heard on the
holy mount. Above the earth, was the Person of the
transfigured Christ, in heavenly glory, and with Him, near
to Him in that glory, were Moses and Elias in holy con-
verse. They are representatives of the sleeping saints who
will be raised, and of the living saints who will be changed
without tasting death. This forms the heavenly depart-
ment of the kingdom. Lower down, on the earth, yet
raised above their fellows, stood Peter, James, and John,
still in mortal bodies—not in resurrection as the heavenly
saints—yet within sight and hearing of the heavenly scene
above. This shows what will be the place of renewed and
restored Israel, the earthly people, in millennial days. The
earthly Jerusalem "lifted up," and safely inhabited (Zech.
14:10), shall bask in the light and glory of the heavenly
city (Is. 40:1; Rev. 21:23, 24). Need we wonder that
Peter, in the midst of such a scene, said, "it is good for us
to be here"—and wanted to erect three tabernacles (booths)
on the hallowed spot. But the time for the celebration of
the Antitype of the Feast of Tabernacles had not come.
They were left with "Jesus Only," as we are still. The
eighth day, "the last great day of the feast," points on a

period beyond millennial times, for these, blessed as they will be, are not the perfect state. Unregenerate man, will still be God's enemy, and there will be a last great outburst of Satanic power, immediately that Satan is loosed from his prison beneath, in which all unregenerate men will share. Then follows the passing away of the heavens and earth—the end of man's history, and the dawn of the eternal day—"the last great day of the feast"—the long Sabbath of Eternity, where, in a new heaven and a new earth, amid all things new, righteousness shall have its dwelling-place, and God shall be *"all in all"*.

> "Beneath Thy touch, beneath Thy smile,
>   New heavens and earth appear;
> No sin their beauty to defile
>   Or dim them with a tear.
>
> Thrice-happy hour, and those thrice-blest
>   Who gather round Thy throne;
> They share the honours of Thy rest,
>   Who have Thy conflict known."

Appendices

A—The Passover

IN Sir Robert Anderson's *Redemption Truths,* he entitles the second chapter, "A New Reading of the Passover." The words, "I will pass over you," which have hitherto been taken to mean the exemption from judgment of those who had sprinkled the blood on the lintel and door-posts, he claims, mean much more. The verb *pasach,* he points out, occurs in three other passages, namely, 2 Sam. 4:1, 1 Kings 18:21, 26, and Isa. 31:5. In the first, it is rendered "become lame"; in the second, *leaping* and *halt* while the third tells of a *passing over* to preserve (R.V.) as a bird her young. After commenting on all these usages of the Word, the author writes:—"And thus it was that He preserved them on that awful night, when the destroyer was abroad, in the land of Egypt. The highest thought suggested by the conventional reading of the passage, is that He spared them : the truth is that He stood on guard, as it were, at every blood-sprinkled door. He became their Saviour. Nothing short of this is the meaning of the Passover."

B—The Lord's Supper

THE perversion of the simple Memorial Feast began shortly after the apostles' time. First, by some claiming ministerial functions, and presiding at the table. By and by, the table with its memorials of a once-offered and forever accepted Sacrifice, whose virtues abide continually, was changed for an altar, before which men acting as priests, offered up to God what at first were known as "sacrificial memorials" of the offering of Christ. These soon became a "mystery," out from which "the Real Presence" was developed, the bread and wine, at the word of a priest, becoming the "true body of Christ," exalted as an object of worship. Such is the idolatry of the Mass, the full-grown blasphemy of Rome. Luther taught that by consecration, "in, with, or under the bread," was the glorified body of the Lord. And Ritualists of the

Anglican Church, are somewhere about halfway between Luther and the Pope, their trend being distinctly towards the latter ; for they claim that the consecrated bread has under its form the presence of the true body, which is to be worshipped—a doctrine Luther never taught. This is the " High Church " theory. The Protestant's " Sacrament " is to many little more than a renewal of " vows," to " keep the commandments," and thereby gain merit for heaven, or in making a fresh start to " do the best they can " to obtain salvation by works. It is a dangerous thing to tamper with, and to add to, or alter in the smallest detail, a Divine institution, which was originally founded by the Lord on the night of His betrayal, and given by Him anew from the throne in the heavens to the Apostle Paul, in abiding form, to be communicated to the Church, and by it continued through the ages, " till He come." To alter for " convenience," or accommodate to " present conditions," any of God's institutions, is to open the door for man's imitations and corruptions. Let us beware !

C—The Fatherhood of God

" UNION in Incarnation," and the common " Fatherhood of God," is the sheet anchor of " Broad Church " teaching. By this all mankind, either by birth or, at baptism, become " God's children," and although some are " prodigal," all must at last be saved. This, which was the teaching of the Oxford " Tractarians," over a century ago, has become the popular doctrine of half the pulpits of Christendom, including some erstwhile " evangelicals," who have left their first faith, being overcome by the temptation to become " up-to-date " preachers," and to pander to the crowd, who supply their emoluments, according to the measure of the pleasure, rather than the profit they get, under such ministry. To these must be added the coming race of budding clerics, who, under the spell of German Neologists, and " Higher Critic " Professors and Principals of Colleges, have had the " Fatherhood " doctrine—which ignores the need of being " born again," and denies the final retribution of the unregenerate, and the Christ-rejector's doom—rubbed into them in their student days, to such an extent, with all the pride and conceit that this glorification of " Old Adam " imparts, that it is a very rare thing to find coming from the pulpits of Presbyterian Scotland—the land of Chalmers, M'Cheyne, and the Bonars—any definite Gospel which tells a sinner how to be saved, or any distinct teaching showing his need of that salvation.

D—The Resurrection Denied

SINCE the day that the Jewish elders " gave large money " to the Roman guard, to circulate the lie that the disciples of the Lord

stole His dead body from the tomb while they were asleep, there
has been a succession of attempts made by " enemies of the
Cross " to deny the Resurrection. The devil does not like it to
be known, that although he put forth all the strength of his power
to crush the Son of God at Calvary and to hold His body in the
grave, he was utterly defeated in the former, and completely
routed in the latter attempt. Wincing under this humiliation,
and enraged at the exaltation of the Prince of Life to the throne
in the heavens, where He awaits the final subjection of His foes
(Psa. 110:1 ; 1 Cor. 15:25),   and from which in His triumph, He
will come to bruise the head of Satan (Rom. 16:20), the adversary
gives his chief attention to making attacks on all that God has
written concerning the glories and triumphs of His Son. Need
we wonder that His resurrection—in which He was " declared the
Son of God in power "   (Rom. 1:4, R.V.)—is a chief object of his
hate. In early times, the Rationalists (1 Cor. 15:35) scoffed at it.
German sceptics, such as Strauss and Renan, denied Christ's
resurrection on other grounds, making it mythical and emblem-
atical, and their disicples, the Rationalist Professors of Oxford,
Edinburgh, and Aberdeen, who have the training of the coming
preachers in their hands, lead them along the same path as far
as they dare, with the result that " Jesus and the Resurrection "
is little heard of in popular preaching.

E—Israel's Restoration

ALTHOUGH the national sin of God's earthly covenant people,
Israel, which culminated in the crucifixion of their Messiah (Acts
2:23), and in the rejection of the Holy Spirit's testimony to Him
as glorified in the heavens   (Acts 7:56), has postponed the fulfilment of the promises made to the fathers, they have not blotted
them out, nor caused the faithfulness of God to fail. The chapters
telling of Israc.'s present unbelief and off-cutting   (Rom. 9-11),
do not close without the assurance, that in spite of their sin, they
shall yet be visited in mercy ; " For," says the inspired writer,
" the gifts and calling of God are not repented of " (Chap. 11:29,
R.V.). Christendom in its pride may despise the Jew, and approp-
riate all the promises of earthly blessing, piously writing—as in
some Bible headlines—above such passages as   Isaiah 11, 32,
" Promises to the Church," and " Blessings of the Gospel," but
they belong by right to the restored and regenerated earthly
people, when in the latter day, they turn to the Lord.

F—Atonement

THE word occurs only once in the A.V. of the New Testament,
namely in Romans 5:11, and there it is a mistranslation. The

R.V. renders it, " We have now received the reconciliation."
Atonement was something given to God to make reconciliation
possible to men, and that " something " was shed blood ; for
" it is the blood that maketh an atonement for the soul " (Lev.
17:11).   Aaron made an atonement " for himself, and for his
household, and for the congregation of Israel." It was, as we are
told, by sprinkled blood on and before the mercy-seat (Lev. 16:
15). The antitype is Christ, " Whom God has set forth to be a
mercy-seat through faith in His blood "—the word used in
Heb. ix. 5 for the ark lid of the tabernacle, and in   Romans 3:25,
for Christ, is the same. And He Himself is the propitiation, as
1 John 2:2, and 4:10, informs us, as well as the propitiatory, the
meeting-place between God and man. All attempts to explain
away the sacrificial and vicarious aspects of our Lord's death, by
making it to be only a supreme act of self-scarifice, in order to
win man back to God, fail. For this leaves sin out of reckoning
altogether, and represents man as only needing moral suasion—
not expiation—to make him right with God.

G—The Accuser in Heaven

IN his *Lectures on Revelation*, Mr. Wm. Lincoln says, " It would
appear as if AFTER the rapture of the Church, the accuser will
still be allowed to be in heaven, and his presence be brooked by
the Lord for three and a half years. For seven years are most
certainly to elapse between the coming of the Lord for His saints
and His subseuqent appearing in glory with them."

H—Israel's Confession of Faith

ALTHOUGH the words of Isaiah 53 may be rightly used by all
who repose in the virtues of the sacrifice of Christ for salvation
and peace, they are primarily those that will be on the lips of the
convicted and confiding earthly people on that day when the veil
will be removed (2 Cor. 3:16), and they shall see in the once
crucified Jesus of Nazareth, their true Messiah and King. Then
as they mourn their sin, each as his personal and family grief,
they shall turn to the " fountain opened " Zechariah 12:10-14;
13:1)   to find in His death the means of their cleansing and
healing.

I—Restitution of all things

" THE Restitution of all things " in Acts 3:21 , has no reference
to man's future destiny, although such a meaning has been read
into the passage. But the context in Acts limits this restitution to
" things which God hath spoken by the mouth of His holy

prophets since the world began." This, as every reader of old Testament prophecy knows, refers to the many passages which speak of times of blessing to the earth, and the earthly people, which will be brought in by judgment on their enemies, not by extended mercy to despisers of grace. Of these " all the prophets " speak in glowing words, but they have not a word to say of " a wider hope " for the ungodly, or a ray of comfort to give to those who now despise the Gospel of Christ and the salvation it proclaims, by holding forth some after-death probation, or evangelization, or universal restoration of all men and demons to God, in virtue of the Cross. That there will be unviersal acknowledgment of Christ's Lordship, Phil. 2:10, informs us, but when reconciliation is in view, as in the kindred passage (Col. 1:20), " things under the earth " are not included in that reconciliation.

THE FEASTS OF

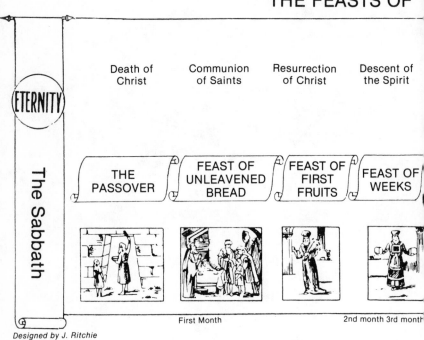

Death of Christ · Communion of Saints · Resurrection of Christ · Descent of the Spirit

ETERNITY

The Sabbath

THE PASSOVER · FEAST OF UNLEAVENED BREAD · FEAST OF FIRST FRUITS · FEAST OF WEEKS

First Month · 2nd month · 3rd month

Designed by J. Ritchie

JEHOVAH. Leviticus 23

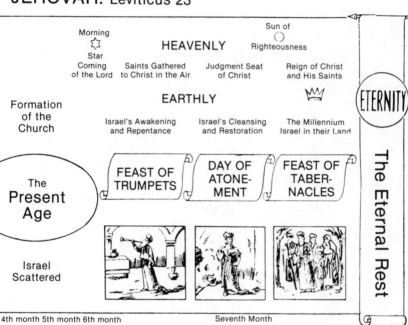

Morning
☆
Star

Sun of
○
Righteousness

HEAVENLY

| Coming of the Lord | Saints Gathered to Christ in the Air | Judgment Seat of Christ | Reign of Christ and His Saints |

EARTHLY

Formation of the Church

| Israel's Awakening and Repentance | Israel's Cleansing and Restoration | The Millennium Israel in their Land |

ETERNITY

The Present Age

| FEAST OF TRUMPETS | DAY OF ATONE-MENT | FEAST OF TABER-NACLES |

The Eternal Rest

Israel Scattered

4th month 5th month 6th month   Seventh Month